BE
BARB

GW00707419

JIM MARKS

A MARTIN BOOK

CONTENTS

Published by Martin Books, a division of Woodhead-Faulkner (Publishers) Ltd, Fitzwilliam House, 32 Trumpington Street, Cambridge CB2 1QY

First published 1988

ISBN 0 85941 438 8

Text © James Marks 1988

Photographs and illustrations © Woodhead-Faulkner (Publishers) Ltd 1988

Printed and bound in Great Britain

PREFACE

For centuries past, one of life's greatest pleasures has been sharing a meal. Today, more people are happily discovering that food alfresco adds an exciting new dimension.

Alchemy, which failed countless mediaeval wizards, has provided the most modest barbecue cook with the means to turn mere meals into mouth-watering feasts. It makes even the most meat-impoverished banger look and taste magic.

Sadly however, magic spells can go awry. My major objective is to impart a few basic rules which with some handy hints, the right equipment, and a little practice, should help the novice conjure up delicious meals at will.

After the sweet taste of success, my hope is that you will try as many dishes in this book as your barbecue equipment will allow. Once captivated by the aroma and tantalizing flavour of barbecued food, and the relaxation and fun connected with it, I hope you will regard barbecuing as a year-round activity. In my book, barbecue time is any time. Remember, food cooked on a barbecue not only looks good, smells good and tastes good but it does you the world of good!

Jim Marks

ACKNOWLEDGEMENTS

The publishers would like to thank the following companies for their help in producing photographs for this book:

p. 29	British Pepper and Spice Ltd
p. 33	Mazola Light Sunflower Oil
p. 37	Mushroom Growers' Association
p. 41	Tabasco Pepper Sauce
p. 49	New Zealand Lamb Promotion Council Ltd
p. 53	Bovril Stock Granules
p. 57, 89	Anchor Foods Ltd
p. 65	U.S. Rice Council
p. 73	Heinz All Seasons Dressings
p. 81	Gale's Honey
p. 85	Sun-Pat Peanut Butter
Back cover	Frank Odell Ltd

Barbecue Hardware and Accessories

Modern barbecuing has inevitably spawned a vast array of barbecuing paraphernalia. Today there are literally dozens of models on offer but almost all use one of two types of fuel: charcoal or gas – that are described below.

Before you shop for a barbecue, settle on the grill capacity that is right for your everyday needs. Remember that for the occasional large barbecue party you can probably borrow an extra barbecue or two from friends and neighbours. It is also worth spending a bit more money for a solid, long-lasting barbecue.

Charcoal-burning Barbecues

The traditional charcoal barbecue remains by far the most popular category, with a wide choice of models.

Small and Portable Barbecues

A few years back, small, fully portable barbecues were purchased mainly because of their low cost. Today, people use them especially for picnics and camping.

Picnic/Camping Barbecues. Ideal for people travelling light. They are small, light, quite cheap and rather basic. The smallest disposable version is ideal for a cyclist or backpacker. They are made up of a shallow foil tray which holds a small quantity of charcoal. A thin wire grill supports the food. Of course, there are larger, not quite so basic models, many of which include a windshield and a small rotisserie. A popular model is the 'brief-case' which folds down to an extremely compact, clean and easy to carry unit.

Hibachi. A very familiar type of barbecue. Rectangular units may come with single, double or triple adjustable grills. Hibachis also feature draught-control vents. If you purchase a cast-iron hibachi, check it for broken parts as they are easily damaged in transit. Less common are the excellent barrel-shape units.

Semi-portable Barbecues

The barbecues below could, if desired, be dis-assembled and taken on holiday, or stay permanently in the garden.

Brazier Barbecues. Most models have screw-in or bolt-on legs that support a fairly shallow, circular fire bowl. Brazier barbecues invariably come with a wind shield (the deeper the better) plus a spit. The food grill is usually adjusted by utilizing slots in the windshield though there are circular grills that rotate freely on the axis and are adjusted by a crank handle. The rotating grill allows you to move the food quickly from 'hot spots' to 'cool spots', making it easier to control potential flare-ups. Preferably, the larger and heavier models should include sturdy wheels for easy manoeuverability and a triangular brace or under-shelf for stability.

Hooded Barbecues. Hooded barbecues provide extra protection against wind, allowing food to cook faster and giving more protection against swirling smoke and added stability for the spit.

Covered Barbecues

For those who aspire to greater and more glorious culinary achievements, a covered barbecue is needed. Charcoal or gas fired, a barbecue that incorporates a lid lets you roast, which gives you much greater scope. The heat reflects off the inside surfaces to cook the food evenly, like in an oven. Some of the recipes in this book can only be used with a covered barbecue. They are marked with an asterisk.

Kettle Barbecues. Like the hibachi, the spherical kettle barbecue is becoming familiar all around the world. Its distinctive cherry shape has a domed lid that sits atop the lower bowl. Some lids are hinged, others are completely separate from the lower bowl. All have adjustable air vents, an ashpan inside or outside the bowl, and most have wheels for mobility. The charcoal grate and the food grill sit well down in the fire-bowl, making it ideal for exposed locations.

Square Kettle Barbecues. This model allows the food grill to be adjusted to various levels and, in the better versions, tilted so that rare to well done steaks can be cooked simultaneously. The hinged lid can also be used as a very effective windshield. Most can also accommodate a rotisserie.

Wagon Barbecues

The name probably derives from the covered wagon made famous by countless Westerns. Their distinctive feature is their impressive size.

Most Wagon barbecues include the 'works'; a rotisserie, warming grills, side-tables, etc. Being rather elaborate, the Wagon is best suited to the pool-side.

Permanent Barbecues

Permanent barbecues make a lot of sense for people who enjoy the fun and food of barbecuing and do it often. For me, a perfect permanent barbecue would include an overhead chimney, a rotisserie, large work surfaces, a warming oven, cupboard space, a cover, good lighting and hot and cold running water. Though of course all this is not essential!

Having decided to build your own barbecue, the most important decision is selecting the site. The barbecue should be partially protected from the wind. The surface is also important, it is well worth paving the area.

DIY barbecue kits have become very popular over the last few years because they are very reasonably priced. You will save even more by using cast-off oven or refrigerator grills.

Obviously, unless you are fairly skilled in brick-laying and metalwork, it is best to keep your design simple and straightforward. Most DIY kit manufacturers offer advice on how to construct brickbuilt free-standing barbecues. Lining the barbecue recess with fire bricks is desirable but very expensive. It is worth looking around for 'over-burnt' house bricks as these will withstand the heat more successfully than standard bricks. When deciding the size of your grill, allow 130 square cm (20 square inches) per serving.

Check-points for Charcoal-burning Barbecues

Here are a few points to bear in mind when shopping for a charcoal-burning barbecue. Not all these points need apply for different barbecues.

➤ Check the stability of the barbecue, remembering that it needs to support several pounds of hot coals and a laden grill. If the barbecue has detachable legs, ensure that they are strong enough and will stay in place. Check the assembly, sometimes a barbecue wobbles simply because of loose nuts and bolts.

➤ Check if the barbecue has a warming grill; it is useful for keeping cooked or partly-cooked food warm. A boon when barbecuing for large numbers.

➤ Check the height of semi-portable barbecues. The grill should be at a comfortable height to work at.

➤ Check if the barbecue has a charcoal grate and air vents in the fire bowl. The grate must be able to withstand intense heat and the air vents should slide easily. Both these features improve lighting and controlling the fire.

➤ Check the nickel chrome plating on the food grill. It should have an even coating. Check for thin or even bare patches.

➤ Check that the bars on the grill are spaced closely enough to hold small sausages and chicken wings.

➤ Check that the food grill slots easily into the windshield, remembering that it will be fully laden.

➤ Check any mechanism for moving the grill. It should move easily, even when fully laden. The handle should be well away from the fire bowl.

➤ Check portable and semi-portable barbecues for wind-shields. Without them, cooking in even a moderate breeze can double the cooking time. The deeper and more enclosing the better.

➤ Check that the rotisserie spit is sturdy and that you will not strip the thumb screws when tightening them up.

➤ Check if the lid fits neatly and that it is not distorted anywhere. Check that the lid's air vents move easily.

Gas Barbecues

Gas barbecues are fast growing in popularity despite the apoplectic mutterings from the die-hard traditionalists. People are realising that gas-barbecued food tastes, looks and smells just as good as that cooked over hot charcoal. Not surprising as the distinctive barbecue flavour is created by the food itself. As the food cooks, the savoury juices fall on the hot bed of fuel. The smoke that rises envelops the food and imparts the distinctive taste, appearance and aroma.

Almost all gas barbecues use cylinders of liquefied petroleum gas (LPG) because it stores easily and can be used at home and away.

Most gas barbecues are the Wagon or Pedestal type, some very elaborate. For extra flexibility and ease, especially if you intend to roast and bake, purchase a twin-burner unit. (Burner control-knobs are easier to use if within easy reach rather than lower down on a pedestal.)

The 'charcoal' in a gas barbecue is volcanic rock, or occasionally ceramic blocks. The gas heats the rock which emits a radiant heat with no change of colour. Because of their technical make-up and solid construction, gas barbecues are more expensive than charcoal-burning ones. However, they have several advantages:

➤ Easy to light – most non-portable units have a push-button spark ignitor.

➤ Ready to use after 5–10 minutes.

➤ Easy to turn off.

➤ Extremely economic to use. The lava rock should not need replacing during the barbecue's lifetime, and the cost of gas is very low.

Gas barbecues vary considerably in the number of British Thermal Units (BTUs) their burners are rated at (sometimes expressed in kilowatts). As a rough guide, divide the total BTUs by the size of the cooking area (in square inches). You want a result of about 100 BTUs per square inch.

You must exercise caution with all types of barbecues. With gas in particular, remember:

➤ Read all the information supplied by the manufacturer.

➤ Do not light with the lid closed.

➤ If you do not have a push-button ignitor, make sure you

have the means of lighting the gas before turning on the supply.

➤ Treat your gas cylinders with respect. Never store or carry them upside down. Keep cylinders away from heat and always use the cylinders in an upright position. Never store cylinders below ground level. Should there be a leak, the gas, being heavier than air, will collect and become explosive. (LPG has a distinctive smell to help in the detection of leaks). *Never* look for a leak with a naked light!

➤ When changing a cylinder, make sure the appliance is switched off.

Check-points for Gas-burning Barbecues

When shopping for a gas barbecue, consider these points:

➤ Check if the barbecue has been passed by the independent Calor Gas Laboratories (BS 5258) or has the approval of the American and Canadian Gas Associations.

➤ Check if the barbecue has an approved gas regulator.

➤ Check if sufficient volcanic rock is provided. This is particularly important, an inadequate supply of rock could greatly reduce the efficiency of the barbecue. Spread the rock evenly over the grate. If 'rock size', or larger gaps appear, juices and fat could fall unchecked onto the burner(s) and most likely create a flare-up.

➤ Check if wheeled barbecues are easy to manoeuvre. Most gas barbecues are rather heavy.

➤ Check if the barbecue has a push-button spark ignition (not normally available with small portable gas barbecues).

➤ Check if the burner controls are in a convenient position.

➤ Check if the lid handle(s) is on the side or front. A handle on the front means that your wrist and lower arm are exposed to the heat while lifting and closing the lid.

➤ Check if it has a warming grill.

Accessories and Tools of the Trade

Cooking Accessories

➤ *Basting Brushes*. You need two – one for brushing sauces, the other for applying oil and fats. Must be made from pure bristle.

➤ *Fork*. Should be long handled with a comfortable grip.

➤ *Knives*. Buy a good quality 'professional' carving knife. Add a sharp paring knife, if possible.

➤ *Skewers*. Ideally flat-bladed, about 5 mm (¼-inch) wide. Hardwood or bamboo skewers are perfect for grilling satay.

➤ *Tongs*. Indispensable. They vary enormously in price and efficiency. A good pair has long handles and a firm, but "soft" jaw to grip food. Avoid tongs with sharp teeth or with jaws that cross over.

➤ *Wire Broilers*. Various shapes and sizes for hamburgers, steaks, and fish. The fish broilers are extremely useful as fish is so fragile when cooked.

➤ *Chopping Board*. The bigger the better. Preferably hardwood or a good quality laminate.

➤ *Foil*. Also indispensable. Buy heavy-duty (usually labelled for freezers and barbecues). Useful for wrapping and covering food, protecting protruding bits of turkey and chicken, crown roast, etc.

➤ *Kitchen Paper*. Always needed to mop up, wipe greasy hands, half-wrap hot sausages, etc.

➤ *Gloves and Apron*. Get good quality gauntlets; wrists and forearms need protection too! Nothing beats a long apron made from good quality cloth with one or two deep pockets in the front.

➤ *Thermometer*. Two types, the round clock-type and the flat arrow-head. Very useful for checking the internal temperature of meat. A false reading occurs if the thermometer touches bone or spit rod.

➤ *Spit, Spit Motor, Spit balance weights.* Most spit-rods that are supplied with the fully portable and semi-portable barbecues are somewhat flimsy. The thumb screws securing the meat tines to the spit-rod should be sturdy enough to be tightened firmly without the threads stripping. A spit rod should be able to support two chickens without deflecting unduly. Most spit motors are battery operated. (The best use two HP2 batteries.) The plastic housing of the cheap motors tends to melt when near hot fuel. A protective 'jacket' of heavy-duty foil helps to prevent this from happening. Harder to find, clockwork-operated spit motors are fine if you remember to keep an eye on them and even more rarely, electrically-operated spit motors. Adjustable balance weights to balance uneven joints are useful but somewhat difficult to find.

Barbecue Accessories

➤ *Vermiculite fire-base.* Used when the fire-bowl lacks air vents.

➤ *Heavy-duty Foil.* Very useful for lining fire-bowls, making drip-trays (see p. 25), and temporary griddles.

➤ *Tongs.* An extra pair is very useful for rearranging hot charcoal.

➤ *Brush.* Small wire brushes, complete with a metal scraper are useful but do tend to clog up fairly quickly. As an alternative, rub over the grill bars with a crumpled-up piece of foil.

➤ *Illumination.* Most barbecue parties are evening affairs, so reasonable lighting is needed for the cook and the guests. Have one or two practical spotlights. Strings of multi-coloured bulbs create a festive atmosphere. A wide variety of wax flares, candles in coloured glass or plastic 'cups' can also set the mood.

➤ *Other useful items.* When barbecuing, you should always have burn lotion and a first aid kit nearby in case of accidents. Bug repellents/killers are always welcomed.

Getting Fired-up

Charcoal

Charcoal for barbecuing is available in two forms, as uniformly pressed briquettes or as natural lumpwood charcoal. No matter the type, always store your charcoal in a dry place. *When burning, charcoal gives off carbon monoxide gas so never cook with it in a confined space.*

Charcoal Briquettes

Briquettes are recommended for two good reasons, they burn about twice as long as natural lumpwood and their uniform size tends to produce an even and more controlled heat.

Different brands vary considerably in their composition and density. The best quality are made from a high percentage of dense hardwoods that have a low resin content (oak, beech and birch). Some brands have a higher mineral content and some also contain excessive amounts of inert 'bulking' materials which provide no additional heat. If dissatisfied with the heat emitted from your briquettes or the length of burn, try other brands until you find one that produces satisfactory results. Instant-lighting charcoal is available in paper bags and cartons. To use, simply light the corners. Do not add to an established fire; the fumes in the early stages of burning will spoil cooking food.

Lumpwood Charcoal

Lumpwood charcoal's advantage is that it is very easy to light. Good quality lumpwood charcoal should be bone-dry and the bag should feel very light. Avoid bags with lots of dust and small pieces at the bottom. The best quality is made from the same hardwoods as for briquettes, and because it takes about 6 tons of green wood to produce 1 ton of charcoal, it is not cheap.

Firelighters

Firelighter Safety

Never use petrol, methylated spirit, lighter fluid, kerosene, naptha or similar volatile liquids to light the charcoal. It is dangerous to you and those standing by.

Never add more starter fluid of any kind to charcoal which has already been ignited – even if the charcoal does not appear to be burning. If you wish to rekindle the fire, use a solid firelighter. If in doubt, it is safer to start the fire again from scratch.

Solid Firelighters

Highly popular with generations of housewives for starting the home fires burning, the familiar solid white block is equally popular for barbecues. A new version comes in a tray containing 20 cubes. Claimed to be smokeless with the added advantage that the remaining cubes stay sealed. However, both the odour and the smoke from the traditional solid firelighter will have dissipated well before the charcoal fire is hot enough to cook food.

Liquid Firelighter

All commercial liquid firelighters for barbecue use are non-volatile but still do not add to a lit fire.

Jellied Alcohol (Lighter Paste)

Relatively expensive, but probably the most convenient starter to take on barbecue picnics. Also known as Lighter Paste, it burns very cleanly with an almost indiscernible flame. Available in cans or sachets.

Charcoal Chimneys

Once purchased, using a chimney is very inexpensive. Having been positioned on the charcoal grate or fire bowl, the chimney, a large open ended metal tube with a handle fixed to one side, is stuffed at the bottom with two or three crumpled sheets of newspaper. It is then filled with charcoal and the paper is lit. When the charcoal has ignited, about 20 minutes, remove the chimney.

13

Gas Torch

Though you have to be on hand for several minutes, a compact Gas Torch operating off a small cartridge of butane gas (like those used by handymen) provides excellent results at a reasonable cost. One advantage over other starters is that a stiff breeze will not snuff out the flame before the charcoal is lit.

Firing Up

For a successful barbecue, a well made fire is essential.

Preparing the Fire bed

Though many barbecues have a fire grate, there are still many that do not, which means that the fire must be laid directly on the base of the barbecue. This restricts air circulation severely. If there are also no air vents, it is difficult to start and keep the fire burning at a steady rate. The following steps can help you.

➤ Line all of the fire bowl with heavy-duty foil, shiny side up. The foil reflects the heat back to the food grill. It also protects the paintwork and makes cleaning and replacing the fire bed easier.

➤ Cover the base of the lined bowl with vermiculite (commercial fire base) about 4 cm (1½ inches) deep. Dry, clean river gravel, about 5 mm (¼ inch) diameter, can also be used. (Replace the vermiculite after about six barbecues or wash and thoroughly dry the gravel.)

Preparing the Charcoal for Cooking

1. Grilling. First build a pyramid-shaped pile of charcoal on the fire grate or fire bowl (fig. 1).

   If using *solid firelighters*, insert two or three pieces well into the lower half of the pyramid. After lighting, the starter will burn for about 15 minutes, depending on the type of barbecue and amount of wind. Carefully check that all pieces have completely burned away before starting to cook. When most of the coals are covered by a grey ash, spread them over the fire grate or fire base.

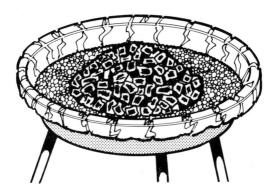

Fig. 1

If using *liquid firelighter*, squirt about 90 ml (3 fl oz) of commercial liquid firelighter on to the cold charcoal. Leave for 50–60 seconds, and then light with a long match or taper. Take care when using a barbecue that has a fire grate and/or air vents in the fire-bowl not to use too much liquid. Excess liquid may drip out of the barbecue and accidentally ignite.

If using *jellied alcohol*, squeeze small amounts of the jelly into cavities near the base of the pyramid. Close and remove the tube. Light the jelly as soon as possible.

If using an *electric starter*, nestle it well into the coals near the base of the pyramid. Switch on the power and leave for 5–8 minutes (do not leave the element on longer than the recommended period as this could cause the element to burn out). Remove the element and reshape the pyramid. The coals should be ready after about 30 minutes.

If using a *gas torch*, arrange the charcoal on the fire grate or fire bed one layer deep and closely together. Light the gas and adjust the flame, and then play the flame slowly over the bed of fuel until grey patches appear on the surface of the coal which glow dully when the flame is on them.

2. Spit-roasting. Build a pile of charcoal on the fire grate or fire base at the rear of the barbecue (fig. 2) and light as described above. Further details concerning the place-

Fig. 2

ment of a drip pan and cooking techniques are given on p. 21.

3. Roasting (only applicable to Covered Barbecues).

Option A (for hotter cooking): Position a drip pan (an old roasting tin can be kept for this purpose) in the centre of the fire grate and arrange an equal amount of coal on each side of the pan. If using a solid firelighter, two pieces per side should be adequate. (Keep an eye on the progress of the two separate fires; should one race away, transfer some hot coals to the cooler side and then adjust the barbecue so that the cooler side gets a better draught.)

Option B (for cooler cooking): Position the drip pan to one side of the fire grate and place the pile of charcoal next to it and light as described as above.

Timing

With all the variables involved – barbecue efficiency, quality of fuel, wind strength and temperature – it is impossible to say exactly how long it takes for the fire to be ready for cooking. For first-time barbecue cooks, err on the generous side. If you want to start cooking at 8 pm, light the fire at around 7 pm. Make a mental note of how the fire looked at around 7.30 pm so that you can gauge when to light the fire for the next barbecue.

How much fuel?

Too often, people use far too much fuel. When laying a fire, they do not seem to take account of the amount of food they wish to cook. Apart from being a considerable waste of money and energy, the excessive heat can easily result in a flare-up (see p. 18) which chars the meat while leaving the inside quite raw.

If you just want to barbecue some burgers and sausages, gauge the area of the grill that will be occupied by the food. Lay a single layer of charcoal (with a small gap between each piece) overlapping the area covered by food by 2.5 cm (1 inch).

Should you wish to use the entire surface of your barbecue, use about 45 pieces of charcoal for a 60 cm (24-inch) diameter unit or about 25 pieces for a 46 cm (18-inch) diameter unit. (Leave 2.5 cm (1 inch) gaps between pieces.)

There are approximately 80 pieces in an average 3 kg (7 lb) bag.

Judging the Fire Temperature

Not many charcoal barbecues come with a heat indicator, but here are two methods you can easily follow for checking if the fire is ready:

➤ Check that at least 80 per cent of the charcoal is covered with grey ash.

➤ Check the temperature by holding your hand, fingers extended and palm down, about 2.5 cm (1 inch) above the food grill. Count how many seconds you can hold the position before the heat forces you to move your hand away.

Hand over fire:	Fire temperature:
2 seconds	Hot
3 seconds	Medium/Hot
4 seconds	Medium
5 seconds	Low

Most food needs cooking at the medium/hot temperature. To estimate the temperature for spit-cooking, hold your hand 7.5–10 cm (3–4 inches) below the spit.

Heat Control

You can control the heat by the following methods:

➤ Lower the food grill for a higher temperature, raise the grill for a lower temperature.

➤ Close the gaps between the charcoal for a higher temperature. Increase the gaps between the charcoal for a lower temperature. (Tapping off excess ash will quickly increase the temperature.)

➤ Open the air vents to increase the draught; the greater the draught the fiercer the heat. To lower the temperature, half close the vents. (Closing the vents completely will help to snuff out live coals in a covered barbecue.)

Flare-ups

The bane of far too many barbecue cooks is a flare-up (a sudden blaze). Some people actually believe that a spectacular flare-up is a part of a cookout because so many books and articles on barbecuing show photographs of flames gaily flickering through the grill bars.

Flare-ups are to be avoided like the plague because they can quickly spoil your food. The worst flare-ups result from the combination of excessive heat and fatty food. Even over a moderate heat, it would be virtually impossible to avoid a flare-up when cooking a full grill of fatty burgers or sausages.

You can control the odd flare-up with a fine water spray directed at the base of the flames (remove the food to a cooler spot on the grill first). Do not cover all of the charcoal grate or fire bowl with fuel. With an open barbecue, once

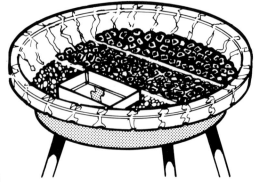

Fig. 3

the charcoal is burning well, set one-third of the base with the charcoal closely together (1 cm (½-inch) gaps), one third set about 5 cm (2 inches) apart and the remaining third empty or occupied by a drip pan (fig. 3). Over the hot spot, you can seal the surfaces of meat before moving it to a moderate heat. 'Park' the cooked or partly-cooked food over the coolest spot while the remaining food finishes.

Tilting the barbecue slightly toward the empty area with the grill bars facing the same direction, some fat will run down the bars to drop off into the drip pan.

With this arrangement, you should be able to rustle up rare, medium and well done steaks to order.

Fire Snuffing

Charcoal, if left on its own, will continue burning until all that is left is ash. Therefore, you should snuff the coal as quickly as possible after cooking. In covered barbecues, the fire can be snuffed by merely closing the lid and all the vents. The coals should be extinguished in about 30 minutes. With open units, transfer the coals to a lidded metal coal-bucket or a pail of water (drying them later). Never pour water over the coals while in the barbecue. This could badly damage the unit.

Barbecue Cooking Techniques

Compared to the past, today's barbecue cooks have a wealth of refined equipment at their disposal, making it easy to match and excel the cook in the kitchen on grilling, roasting and spit-roasting. The barbecue cook is alone in being able to tackle the satisfying technique of 'smoke cooking'.

With the barbecue cooking techniques on the following pages, you can flex as many of your culinary muscles as you like, from the simple burger to something more exotic, such as Barbecued Leg of Lamb Provençal (p. 44).

Grill Cooking

Grilling food on an open barbecue is certainly the most

popular and widely practised method of barbecue cooking.

Grilling requires constant attendance so anything that can be cooked within 30–40 minutes is a candidate for this technique: steaks, chops, chicken portions, hamburgers, sausages, kebabs, fish steaks and whole fish or even thicker butterflied joints.

Grilling Procedure

➤ When your fire is at the correct temperature (see p. 17), lightly knock some of the ash off just before starting to cook.

➤ Rub a little fat on the food grill or brush on some cooking oil. Lubricating the grill helps to prevent the food from sticking.

➤ If possible, adjust the food grill 5–8 cm (2–3 inches) above the hot coals. Sear meat at this level for a minute or so. Raise the grill 10–15 cm (4–6 inches) above the coals and continue cooking. For Gas Barbecues, you can simply adjust the heat from the high setting to low to medium.

Notes on Grilling

➤ Brush a little oil or butter, seasoned if you like, over one surface of the meat. Place that side down on the grill. Lightly baste the second side just before turning.

➤ Apply thick basting sauces or glazes during the final few minutes of cooking. If it is put on too early, the meat may burn and blacken, especially over a moderately high cooking temperature.

➤ Never crowd the grill with fat-loaded foods such as hamburgers and sausages. It will inevitably cause a massive flare-up and a thick pall of smoke. If this happens with no spare room on the grill surface, immediately remove all the food from the grill.

➤ Marinating the meat for a few hours tenderises and flavours the meat.

➤ You can thaw frozen meat while it marinates. Keep the meat in the marinade until it is completely defrosted.

Skewer Grilling

The beauty of skewer grilling is that you can let your imagination run wild and combine any meat, vegetable or fruit you like. Marinating the food gives you even more scope.

Skewers come in a wide range of lengths, most made from stainless steel. Those with flat or square-section blades ensure that the food turns with the skewer. The two-prong variety is also very effective though hard to find.

The basic cooking procedure is the same as for grilling (see p. 20). These tips will help you get the best results from skewer grilling:

➤ Brushing the skewers with oil before threading on the food will prevent sticking.

➤ When impaling chunks of fish, leave the skin intact; this helps to hold the flesh together while cooking.

➤ For even cooking, either make up kebabs with food that has similar cooking times or part-cook slower cooking foods so that the grilling times will be roughly equal.

Spit-roasting

It requires more preparation work than the other techniques but spit-roasting has considerable appeal, reflected in the fact that on most barbecues you can mount a rotisserie, while on many models the basic spit-roasting equipment is a standard feature.

There are numerous accessories for spit-roasting small food; flat and cylindrical spit baskets can hold several chicken drumsticks for example, and there are attachments for supporting four to eight kebab skewers. However, spit-roasting is best for large pieces of meat, poultry or large whole fish.

Spit-roasting procedure

Prepare the fire bed for spit-roasting (p. 15).

It is important that the spit goes through the centre of the food so that the spit is evenly balanced. Before fully tightening the spit-forks (tines), slowly rotate the spit. If there is no tendency for the laden spit to roll suddenly from any position, the balance is good. With practise, you should be able to centre the food regardless of its shape. After balancing the food, the spit-forks should be fully tightened, preferably with pliers if the thumb screws will stand up to the pressure.

Notes on Spit-roasting

➤ Poultry and game birds should be securely tied into a compact shape; cover any protruding wing tips or bones with foil to prevent them from charring.

➤ If the drip pan is flush with the fire bed, fill the pan three-quarters full with water or left-over beer or wine. You can then use the liquid as a savoury baste, adding various appropriate herbs.

➤ Unless marinated, the joint should be brushed with oil once mounted on the spit.

➤ When spit-roasting boneless rolled roasts, particularly pork, it is recommended that a meat thermometer is used to ensure that the roast is fully cooked through before serving. (Insert the shaft of the thermometer into the roast at a slight angle, so that the tip rests in the centre of the thickest portion, avoiding the spit rod.)

➤ If planning to impale more than one piece of meat on the same spit, leave room between them so that the heat can reach all surfaces.

➤ When cooking two chickens at once, you might need to extend the fire-bed at each side so that all of the chicken will be cooked at the same time.

Roasting

It is possible and practical to use a covered barbecue for fast cooking steaks, chops and hamburgers etc., but covered barbecues are generally used for roasting joints and whole birds, casseroles and baking bread, pies, cakes, pizzas, etc. This versatile technique of roasting allows the barbecue to be used very much like a domestic oven. The enhanced appearance, natural succulence and flavour of roasts barbecued this way persuades many cooks to use their covered barbecues year-round. Christmas is an opportune time to give the oven much needed space by roasting the turkey in the barbecue.

Roasting Procedure

Set up the fire bed and position a drip pan (fig. 4). Place the joint over the pan. The food is cooked from the heat reflecting off the barbecue lid and fire bowl.

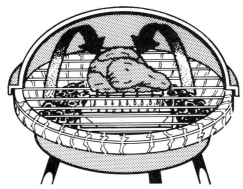

Fig. 4

Roasting in a Gas Barbecue

This is very straightforward if using a twin-burner unit. Light one of the burners. Position a drip pan under the food grill of the unlit side and place the joint over the pan. (Follow the manufacturer's instructions concerning the use of the barbecue in this way.) If the twin-burner gas barbecue is small, you may need to spin the meat 90° roughly half way through to ensure even cooking.

If you have a single burner unit, follow these instructions:

➤ Place the smallest pieces of volcanic rock closely together in the centre of the grate.

➤ Place a shallow steel roasting tin on top of the small pieces of rock. The tin (drip pan) should be large enough to catch almost all of the fat. (Some gas units have very little space between the rocks and the food grill. In this

23

case, rest the grill straight on top of the drip pan. Check that the barbecue lid can be closed or almost fully closed.)

➤ Fill the drip pan three-quarters full with water or left-over beer or wine. Bearing in mind that the burner is situated directly under the drip pan it will be necessary to check the amount of liquid in the pan periodically. Top up carefully with a kettle or small watering can. Do not pour liquid into a drip pan that only contains hot fat.

Notes on Roasting

➤ Using a rib-rack in a covered barbecue will greatly increase the barbecue's capacity when cooking spare-ribs (sectioned or whole), chops, and chicken quarters.

➤ Place packages of foil-wrapped vegetables around the joint during the final period of cooking (see p. 69).

➤ Straight after removing the meat and vegetables, place a raw fruit tart in the covered barbecue. The tart should be ready shortly after you have finished the main course.

Smoke-cooking

Do not confuse smoke-cooking and smoking (smoke-curing). Smoke-curing is a highly skilled, slow process, working with temperatures as low as 10°C/50°F and can take several days to complete. Its primary aim is to preserve meat and fish. There are now portable smokers available which let you get closer to the 'real thing'. These cylindrical-shaped units have a close fitting lid, one or two grills to support food, a grate or fire bowl to support the charcoal and aromatic smoking woods, and a pan to hold water or other liquid between the grill and grate.

Smoke-cooking on the other hand, is a 'hot' smoking process done to impart a richer colour and a more tangy flavour to the food. You can smoke-cook with any covered barbecue and the cooking times are generally the same as for regular barbecuing.

Poultry, ham, spare-ribs, pork, lamb, venison, kidneys, sausages and a variety of fish such as salmon, trout, mackerel, eel and oysters are excellent for smoke-cooking.

The smoke is produced from aromatic wood, such as hickory and mesquite or indigenous hardwoods such as oak, cherry, beech, apple, alder, vine, sycamore and poplar. Do not use pine or other resinous softwoods; these will have an unpleasant effect on the food. If desired, you can enhance the pleasant fragrance by adding sprigs of rosemary or thyme. Soak the wood for an hour or two before putting it on the hot coals or rocks.

Experience will tell you when and how much wood to apply for the result you want. As a rough guide, a chunk of hickory the size of an egg applied to the hot coals half way through roasting a 1½ kg (3 lb) chicken should turn the chicken to a darkish mahogany colour and just a delicate smoked flavour.

The next time you smoke-cook, you can apply more at an earlier stage for more flavour if you wish.

Notes on Smoke-cooking

➤ Place an open pot of baked beans alongside the joint and it will take on a pleasant smoky flavour. Stir occasionally.

➤ Brush a glaze over the meat about 10–15 minutes before the end of the cooking. This will intensify the colour and will impart an attractive lustre. Do not apply the glaze too soon or it will caramelise and burn.

Barbecuing Hints and Tips

➤ An aluminium foil drip pan plays an important role when roasting and spit-roasting. Making one to size is a very simple matter as shown by fig. 5.

Tear off a strip from a 46 cm (18-inch) roll of heavy-duty aluminium foil that is about 10 cm (4 inches) longer than the length of the pan you require. Fold the foil in half lengthwise. Double-fold the edges to provide side walls of about 2.5 cm (1 inch). Pull out the corners and fold back tightly against the sides. This will give you a

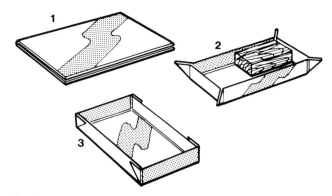

Fig. 5

leak-proof tray approximately 13 cm (5 inches) wide with sides 2.5 cm (1 inch) high.

➤ On a covered barbecue, occasionally wipe the underside of the lid while it is still warm. This keeps the grease from building up.

➤ Prior to grilling spare-ribs or pork cutlets, seal them with 2 tablespoons of water in a foil package and heat in a moderate oven (or roast on a covered barbecue) for about 45 minutes. This will render out a lot of the fat, reducing the possibility of flare-up and greatly shortening the cooking time.

➤ Always use tongs to turn flat meats. A fork could pierce the meat, allowing precious juices to escape.

➤ Wrapping a large whole fish in clean chicken wire (burn off the galvanised coating beforehand) keeps it intact and easier to handle when spit-roasting or grilling.

BEEF RECIPES

Hot n' Spicy Burgers

Serves 4

500 g (1 lb) finely minced chuck steak
1 small onion, chopped finely
¼ tsp dry mustard
2 tsp soy sauce
1½ tbs chilli sauce
2 tsp horseradish sauce
1 tbs hot and tangy barbecue spice
4 soft rolls

Lightly mix together the first 7 ingredients and shape the mixture into 4 burgers.

Cook the hamburgers on the grill over a high heat, turning once, for approximately 20 minutes or until nicely browned. Toast the rolls during the last few minutes of cooking and serve the burgers in the rolls.

Cheese and Bacon Burgers

Serves 6

750 g (1½ lb) finely minced chuck steak
1½ tbs mild and fruity barbecue spice
¾ tsp salt
4 tbs Cheddar cheese, grated
3 bacon rashers, streaky or back
6 soft rolls
a pinch of black pepper

Lightly mix together the minced steak, barbecue spice, salt and pepper. Gently shape the mixture into 6 burgers and cook over a high heat for approximately 20 minutes, turning once. Shortly after turning, sprinkle the grated cheese on the burgers and start grilling the bacon rashers. When crisp, dice the rashers and scatter them over the melting cheese. Toast the rolls during the last few minutes of cooking and serve the burgers in them.

Jim's Tasty-tater Burgers

Serves 6

750 g (1½ lb) finely minced chuck steak
1 medium onion, chopped finely
½ tsp garlic salt or 1 tsp salt
1 large baking potato
50 g (2 oz) butter, mixed with 1½ tbs original barbecue spice
6 soft rolls
freshly ground black pepper

Lightly mix together the minced steak, onion, garlic salt or salt, and pepper. Lightly shape into 6 burgers, approximately 1 cm (½-inch) thick.

Cut the potato into 6 slices about 3–5 mm (⅛–¼ inch) thick, discarding the outer slices. Cook the burgers over a high heat for approximately 20 minutes, turning once. After turning, place the slices of potato on the grill and spread with the barbecue-spiced butter. Turn the potato slices over and grill for 4–5 minutes. Turn the slices over and baste and grill the uncooked sides for a further 4–5 minutes. Toast the rolls and place the burgers in them, topping each with a slice of tasty-tater.

Hot n' Spicy Burgers
Cheese and Bacon Burgers
Jim's Tasty-tater Burgers

Barbecued Beef Bites

Makes about 40

5 cm (2-inch) piece of fresh ginger root, peeled and sliced
2 small onions, chopped
1 garlic clove, minced
125 g (4 oz) sugar
250 ml (8 fl oz) soy sauce
8 small dried chilli peppers or 1 tsp chilli powder
2 tbs red wine vinegar
4 tsp cornflour
150 ml (¼ pint) water
1 kg (2 lb) sirloin of beef, cut into bite-size pieces

Combine the first 7 ingredients. Heat in a small pan for about 20 minutes, or until slightly thick. Blend the cornflour with the water. Gradually add to the sauce and stir continuously until the mixture is clear and has thickened. Strain the sauce, pressing out all the juices. Discard the pulp and allow the sauce to cool. Add the beef pieces and marinate for approximately 2 hours. Thread two or three pieces of meat on each oiled skewer and cook over a medium heat, turning often, for about 10 minutes or until the beef is cooked to your liking.

Chinese Beef Snake

Serves 8 **(Pictured on front cover)**

750 g (1½ lb) boneless sirloin steak, 2.5 cm (1-inch) thick
300 ml (½ pint) dry red wine
6 tbs soy sauce
4 tbs sake or sherry
50 g (2 oz) brown sugar
1 tsp ground ginger
1 small garlic clove, minced
1 tbs sunflower oil

Partially freeze the meat, and then cut it across the grain in thin, slanting slices about 3 mm (⅛-inch) thick. Place the slices in a shallow pan.

Combine the rest of the ingredients and mix well. Pour over the steak strips and marinate for about 1 hour. Drain and thread the strips of meat, snake-fashion, on to 15–20 cm (6–8-inch) oiled skewers.

Cook over a medium heat for just 1–2 minutes on each side, basting with the marinade.

John Wayne's Short Ribs

Serves 4–6

1.25 kg (3 lb) lean short ribs
150 ml (¼ pint) dry red wine
1 tbs Worcestershire sauce
300 ml (½ pint) tomato juice
2 garlic cloves, minced
¼ tsp ground cloves
¼ tsp dried thyme
1 tsp dry mustard
1 tbs brown sugar
1 tsp salt
1 small onion, chopped finely
3 tbs sunflower oil

Place the ribs in a shallow dish. Combine all the marinade ingredients, except the onion and oil, and pour over the meat. Place the dish in the refrigerator and leave for 24–48 hours; turn the meat occasionally.

Leave the meat at room temperature for 2–3 hours before cooking. About 30 minutes before cooking the ribs, add the onion and oil to the marinade.

Lightly grease the grill and set it 10–13 cm (4–5 inches) above a high heat. Turn and baste the ribs every 5–10 minutes. Cook the ribs for 30–40 minutes, or until done to your liking. You can boil up any extra marinade and serve it over the ribs.

Stuffed Rump Steak with Parsley Butter

Serves 4

1 tsp finely chopped shallot or onion
sunflower oil
125 g (4 oz) open mushrooms, wiped and chopped finely
2 tsp finely chopped parsley
1 tsp finely chopped thyme
1 rounded tbs cooked ham, chopped finely
1 tbs fresh breadcrumbs
750 g (1½ lb) rump steak, about 4 cm (1½ inches) thick
15 g (½ oz) butter
a squeeze of lemon juice
salt
freshly ground black pepper

To prepare the stuffing, first soften the chopped shallot or onion in a little sunflower oil. Add the chopped mushrooms, half of the parsley, and thyme. Cover and cook over a medium heat for about 5 minutes. Add the ham, breadcrumbs, salt and pepper. Lightly mix, and then turn out and leave to cool.

Slit the steak on one side to form a deep pocket. Push the stuffing well into the pocket and close the opening with a trussing needle and fine string or a fine skewer.

Brush the steak with the sunflower oil and cook over a medium to high heat for about 4–5 minutes on each side, or until cooked to the desired degree. Before serving, remove the string or skewer.

To prepare the parsley butter, melt the butter and when it is light brown in colour, add the rest of the parsley and the lemon juice. Pour the parsley butter over the steak just before serving. To serve, cut in 1 cm (½-inch) slices.

Stuffed Rump Steak with Parsley Butter

Steak and Blue

Serves 4–6

1 × 750 g (1½ lb) flank steak
175 ml (6 fl oz) french salad dressing
3 tbs butter, softened
75 g (3 oz) blue cheese
1 tbs finely chopped chives
1 garlic clove, minced
1 tbs fresh rosemary, chopped, or 1 tsp dried rosemary
a pinch of dried oregano or dried basil
1 tbs brandy (optional)

Place the steak in a shallow dish and pour over the salad dressing. Turn the steak two or three times, then cover the dish and place it in a refrigerator for at least 3–4 hours, or overnight. Blend the softened butter, blue cheese, chives, garlic, rosemary, and oregano or basil. Add the brandy, if desired. If making the blue cheese butter in advance, keep it in the refrigerator.

Lift the steak from the marinade and drain briefly. Cook over a high heat to the required degree, about 4–5 minutes per side if you like your steak rare.

After transferring the steak to a warm platter, cut it across the grain in thin, slanting slices. Spoon a portion of blue cheese butter over each serving.

PORK RECIPES

Barbecued Ham Steaks

Serves 6

3 tbs butter, melted
6 tbs dry sherry
6 tbs pineapple juice
1 tbs dry mustard
1 tsp ground cloves
1 tsp paprika
1 garlic clove, minced
2 tbs brown sugar
6 × 1 cm (1/2-inch) thick cooked ham slices
6 slices fresh or canned pineapple or 6 canned apricot halves

For the marinade, combine the melted butter, sherry, pineapple juice, mustard, cloves, paprika, garlic and brown sugar. Slash the edges of the ham about every 2.5 cm (1 inch) to prevent curling. Marinate the ham for 3–4 hours, turning several times. Grill over a low to medium heat for about 10 minutes; baste frequently with the marinade and turn occasionally. Place the pineapple slices on the grill for the last 5 minutes, basting occasionally with the marinade and turning two or three times. If using the apricot halves, place these on the grill for the last 3–4 minutes, basting occasionally with the marinade. Serve the ham with the fruit immediately.

Mushroom, Bacon and Green Pepper Kebabs

Serves 6

12 rashers prime streaky bacon
1 medium–large green pepper
12 closed cup mushrooms, wiped
75 g (3 oz) butter, softened
salt and pepper

De-rind the bacon rashers and roll them up. De-seed the pepper and cut it into 12 pieces. Plunge the pepper pieces into boiling water and remove immediately; drain thoroughly.

Alternate pieces of green pepper, mushroom, and bacon rolls on oiled skewers.

Spread the softened butter over each kebab, season, and cook over a medium heat, turning occasionally, about 5–6 minutes.

Mushroom, Bacon and Green Pepper Kebabs

Gingered Ribs

Serves 6–8

150 ml (¼ pint) tomato ketchup
300 ml (½ pint) tomato purée
1 tbs Worcestershire sauce
50 g (2 oz) brown sugar
3 tbs wine vinegar
1 medium-size onion, chopped finely
1 slice of lemon
1 garlic clove, minced
1 tsp salt
½ tsp chilli powder
½ tsp celery salt
¼ tsp dry mustard
⅛ tsp freshly ground black pepper
2 tbs preserved ginger, chopped finely
2.75 kg (6 lb) lean spare-ribs

Combine all the ingredients except the meat in a pan and heat gently. Cover and simmer for 20 minutes, stirring occasionally. If spit-roasting, thread the complete rib sections on to the spit, snake fashion. If grilling, cut the ribs into four rib sections and place on a grill set 10–15 cm (4–6 inches) above the fire. Cook over a medium heat; turn and baste the ribs frequently for 1¼–1½ hours. The ribs are cooked when the meat pulls away from the end of the bones.

Plummy-flavoured Spare-ribs

Serves 8

2 garlic cloves, crushed
1 medium onion, chopped finely
3 tbs red wine vinegar
3 tbs sunflower oil
300 ml (½ pint) dry red wine
125 g (4 oz) red plum jam
3 tbs soy sauce
about 3.5 kg (8 lb) lean spare-ribs, in uncut slabs

Combine all the ingredients except the meat in a small pan and heat gently. Simmer for 5 minutes and allow to cool. Divide the spare-ribs in two to four rib sections. Place a large plastic bag in a large roasting tin and put the ribs in the bag. Pour in the marinade and seal with a twist-tie. Refrigerate for 12–24 hours, turning the bag occasionally.

Reserving the marinade, briefly drain the spare-ribs and place them on a lightly greased grill set 10–15 cm (4–6 inches) above a medium heat. Baste and turn the ribs continuously to ensure even colouring and flavouring, and to prevent the ribs charring. Cook for about 1–1¼ hours, or until the meat pulls away from the bone.

Plum marinade is equally good with beef or lamb ribs.

Bali Pork Satay

Serves 6

6 tbs chutney
3 tbs tomato ketchup
2 tbs sunflower oil
6 dashes Tabasco Pepper sauce
1 tbs soy sauce
1 kg (2 lb) boneless pork loin, cut into 2.5 cm (1-inch) cubes
75 g (3 oz) salted peanuts, chopped very finely

Purée the chutney in a blender until smooth or finely chop it. Turn it into a bowl and add the tomato ketchup, sunflower oil, Tabasco sauce and soy sauce. Add the meat to the mixture, stir, and leave to marinate for several hours, or overnight in a refrigerator, turning the meat over once or twice. Put the finely chopped peanuts on a plate. Impale the meat on six oiled skewers and barbecue over a medium heat for about 12–15 minutes. Turn the skewers occasionally to ensure even browning. When cooked, immediately roll the meat in the peanuts to coat all sides.

Bali Pork Satay

Spicy Glazed Ham*

Serves 25–30

5–6 kg (12–14 lb) cooked boneless gammon
4 tbs oyster sauce
2 tbs dry sherry
2–3 tbs whole cloves

Using a sharp knife, remove the gammon rind and score the fat in a diamond pattern. Combine the oyster sauce and dry sherry. Rub the scored surface of the ham with the mixture, and stick a single clove into the centre of each diamond. Insert a meat thermometer in the centre of the ham and roast over a medium heat for about 2½ hours. Leave the ham for 15–20 minutes before serving.

Heating ham to the recommended internal temperature (see p. 92) only requires a moderate heat. If you do not have a meat thermometer, allow 8–10 minutes/500 g (1 lb). Too high a temperature could spoil the glaze.

Sweet and Hot Pork Chops

Serves 6

6 tbs clear honey
6 tbs Dijon mustard
¼ tsp chilli powder
¼ tsp onion salt
¼ tsp garlic salt
6 × 2.5 cm (1-inch) thick loin pork chops

Combine all the ingredients but the meat. Spoon over the pork chops, cover, and leave in a cool place for 4–6 hours.

Reserving the marinade, drain the chops. Place them on a lightly greased grill set about 10–15 cm (4–6 inches) above a high heat and baste occasionally with the marinade. Cook for 15–20 minutes on each side, or until no pink shows.

Spit-roasted Loin of Pork

Serves 6–8

2 garlic cloves, chopped finely
1 tbs finely chopped fresh rosemary leaves or 1 tsp dried
  rosemary
¼ tsp freshly ground black pepper
1 tsp salt
about 1.75 kg (4 lb) loin of pork

Crush and mix in a mortar the garlic, rosemary, pepper and salt. With a small, sharp knife, make deep incisions in the meat, three at each end of the loin and 6–8 through the skin, or through the scores in the skin if you want ribbed crackling. Insert some of the rosemary and garlic mixture in the incisions and sprinkle the outside of the loin with more salt and pepper.

Position the meat on the spit with a drip pan under the meat to catch the juices for a gravy (see p. 22). Cook slowly over a medium heat, allowing about 25 minutes/500 g (1 lb) or until a meat thermometer reads 90°C/190°F.

LAMB RECIPES

Barbecued Leg of Lamb Provençal*

Serves 8–10

2.25–2.75 kg (5–6 lb) leg of lamb
3 garlic cloves, each sliced in three
12 anchovy fillets
75 g (3 oz) butter, softened, plus 1 tbs
4 medium-size tomatoes
15 g (½ oz) Tarragon and Parsley Butter (see p. 90)
150 ml (¼ pint) stock, made from 1 tbs chicken stock granules
3 shallots, chopped finely
1 tbs plain flour
2 gherkins, chopped finely
1 tbs tomato purée
salt and pepper

Slit the surface of the meat evenly in 9 places and insert the slivers of garlic. Cut 6 of the anchovy fillets into 4 pieces about 2.5 cm (1-inch) long, and lard the joint with them. Spread the softened butter evenly over the surface of the joint and roast over a medium heat for about 1½ hours. Baste occasionally with the butter. For medium-rare meat, the meat thermometer should reach 60–65°C/140–145°F.

Skin the tomatoes and cut them in half vertically. Place the tomato halves alongside the joint during the last 4 minutes of cooking. When the lamb is cooked, set it on a hot dish and arrange the tomatoes, cut side down, around it. Cut 4 of the anchovy fillets into four and place two of these in a cross over each tomato half and put a knob of parsley butter on top.

To prepare the sauce, pour off any surplus fat from the drip pan and deglaze it with 2–3 tablespoons of the stock. Boil it up by either turning the gas control knob to high or by lowering the grill to its lowest setting. If necessary, position the drip pan directly on the hot coals. Finely chop the remaining 2 anchovy fillets. In a saucepan, lightly brown the chopped shallots in 1 tbs of the butter, stir in the flour, and then add the chopped anchovy fillets, gherkins, tomato purée and the remaining stock, and season to taste. Bring the mixture to the boil and simmer for about 4 minutes, and then add the gravy from the drip pan. Stir well and pour the sauce into a warmed sauce boat. Serve separately with the lamb.

Brochettes of Kidney

Serves 4

125 ml (4 fl oz) olive oil
6 tbs red wine
1 tsp dried thyme or a few sprigs of fresh thyme
8 lamb's kidneys, skinned and split, with the white membrane removed
12 cubes of lamb's liver, with the ducts removed
chopped parsley
salt and freshly ground black pepper

Combine the olive oil, red wine, thyme and salt and pepper. Pour over the kidneys and liver and marinate for 2–3 hours.

Thread the slightly drained kidneys (kept open with a big stitch of fine string) and liver alternately on four oiled skewers, and cook for 3–4 minutes on each side over a medium to high heat, basting with the marinade throughout. Be careful not to overcook or they will become tough.

Serve the brochettes on a bed of boiled rice and garnish with the chopped parsley.

Mint Jelly Rolled Lamb*

Serves 4

1 large boned breast of lamb, about 750 g (1½ lb)
75 g (3 oz) fresh white breadcrumbs
½ tsp concentrated mint sauce
grated rind and juice of 1 lemon
1 egg, beaten
mint jelly
salt and pepper

Season the boned breast of lamb. Mix together the fresh breadcrumbs, mint sauce, lemon rind and juice and enough of the beaten egg to produce a fairly stiff mixture. Spread evenly over the cut side of the lamb. Roll the lamb tightly and tie securely with strong string about every 2.5 cm (1 inch) along the roll.

Roast over a medium heat for 1¼–1½ hours. Spread a thin layer of mint jelly over the roll during the last 5 minutes cooking time. Leave the lamb for 10 minutes before carving into slices.

Turkish Kebabs

Serves 6–8

1 kg (2 lb) finely minced lamb
125 g (4 oz) onion, minced finely
3 eggs
1 tsp whole thyme
2 tsp salt
1 garlic clove, minced
sunflower oil

Combine the minced lamb, onion, eggs, thyme, salt and garlic; mix well. Chill the mixture until firm, about 20 minutes. Form the meat into torpedo-shaped pieces about

7.5 cm (3 inches) long and 2.5 cm (1 inch) in diameter. Thread two to three lengthways on oiled skewers (preferably flat-bladed). Brush with the sunflower oil and grill over a high heat for 8–10 minutes, turning to brown all sides.

Herb-charred Butterflied Leg of Lamb

Serves 6–8

1 tbs fresh rosemary or 1 tsp dried rosemary
1 tbs minced dried onion
1 tbs dried whole marjoram
1 large bay leaf, crumbled finely
1/4 tsp ground ginger
1 tsp salt
2 tbs wine vinegar
2 tbs marmalade
300 ml (1/2 pint) dry wine, white or red
150 ml (1/4 pint) stock made from 3 tbs chicken stock granules
2.25–2.75 kg (5–6 lb) leg of lamb, boned and butterflied

Combine all the ingredients except the meat in a pan and heat gently for 20 minutes, stirring occasionally. Slash any thicker areas of the meat. Brush the sauce over the entire surface of the lamb.

Set the grill about 15 cm (6 inches) above a medium heat. Place the meat on the grill with the fat side (uncut surface) up. Baste frequently with the remaining sauce and turn the meat occasionally. Cook for about 50 minutes, or until done to your liking.

When cooked, the butterflied leg of lamb should have a somewhat crusty surface. To serve, slice the lamb thinly across the grain.

Note: to butterfly, cut down the length of the inside of the leg. Cut around the bone and remove.

Lamb Leg Steaks

Serves 4

4 × 2 cm (¾-inch) thick lamb leg steaks
150 ml (¼ pint) sunflower oil
6 tbs lemon juice
1 tsp salt
1 tsp oregano
1 medium-size onion, chopped finely
⅛ tsp black pepper
1 tbs chopped fresh parsley

Place the leg steaks in a shallow dish. Combine the rest of the ingredients and pour over the meat. Marinate overnight in the refrigerator or for a minimum of 4 hours at room temperature.

Grill over a high heat, basting with the marinade a few times, for about 6–7 minutes on each side, or until done to your liking.

Lamb Leg Steaks
Seekh Kebabs

Seekh Kebabs

Makes 8–10 small kebabs

1 medium-size onion, chopped finely
1 tsp garam masala
1/2 tsp ground poppy seeds
1/2 tsp ground turmeric
1/2 tsp chilli powder
1 garlic clove, crushed with a pinch of salt
80 ml (2 1/2 fl oz) plain yogurt
1 tbs lemon juice
750 g (1 1/2 lb) loin or leg of lamb, cut into 2.5 cm (1-inch) cubes
50 g (2 oz) butter, melted
salt

In a bowl, mix together the onion, garam masala, ground poppy seeds, turmeric, chilli powder, garlic, and salt. Stir in the yogurt and the lemon juice. Marinate the cubes of lamb in this mixture for at least 4 hours, or overnight in the refrigerator. Thread the cubes of meat on oiled skewers, ensuring that there is a small gap left between each cube. Brush the meat with the melted butter and cook over a medium to high heat, turning a few times until the meat is tender and evenly browned, about 12–15 minutes.

Serve with chapatis or stuffed into a pitta bread pocket.

POULTRY AND GAME RECIPES

Tandoori Chicken *

Serves 4

75 g (3 oz) butter, melted
½ tsp ground nutmeg
½ tsp ground cinnamon
½ tsp ground coriander
juice of 1½ lemons
1.25 kg (3 lb) chicken
1 small onion
4 garlic cloves
1 cm (½-inch) piece of fresh ginger root, peeled and chopped
1 tsp ground cumin
½ tsp chilli powder
1 tsp salt
150 ml (¼ pint) yogurt

For the tandoori basting sauce, combine the melted butter, nutmeg, cinnamon, ½ tsp of the coriander, and ⅓ of the lemon juice. Mix well and set aside.

Pierce the chicken all over with the point of a skewer. Grind the onion, garlic and ginger together in a blender or pestle and mortar. Add the remaining spices and seasoning and mix thoroughly. Beat the yogurt in a bowl until it is smooth; add the spice paste and the rest of the lemon juice to it and stir until well combined. Rub the mixture over the chicken and marinate it in the refrigerator for at least 4 hours or overnight.

Roast the chicken over a medium to high heat, basting frequently with the tandoori sauce, for about 1½ hours or until the juices run clear when the chicken thigh is pierced with a skewer.

Crunchy-coated Chicken

Serves 4

8 chicken thighs or drumsticks
2 tbs chicken stock granules
2 egg yolks
2 tbs single cream or top of the milk
150 g (5 oz) dry breadcrumbs
3 tsp mixed dried herbs
4 tbs plain flour
salt and freshly ground black pepper

Remove the skin from the chicken. In a small bowl, combine the chicken stock granules, egg yolks and cream; mix well. Mix the breadcrumbs with the mixed herbs and put on a plate or on greaseproof paper. Place the flour on another plate or piece of greaseproof paper.

Season the chicken with salt and pepper, and then roll each piece in the flour, coating evenly. Dip the chicken into the egg mixture evenly, and then roll them firmly in the breadcrumbs. Chill the chicken for 2–3 hours or freeze for about 20 minutes. This sets the coating for easier cooking and also allows the chicken to absorb the flavours.

Grill over a medium heat for about 30 minutes, turning the joints every few minutes so that the coating does not char.

Gene Krupa's Drumsticks

Serves 6

12 chicken drumsticks
125 g (4 oz) cream cheese
12 rashers streaky bacon
sunflower oil
salt and pepper

Using a short, sharp knife, make an incision in the fattest part of each drumstick and fill the slit with cream cheese. Season, and then wrap a rasher of bacon around each drumstick. Secure the bacon with wooden cocktail sticks which have been soaked in water.

Cook over a medium to high heat, basting frequently with the sunflower oil, for about 10 minutes each side.

Chicken with Smoky-bacon Glaze*

Serves 4

1.25 kg (3 lb) chicken
2 slices smoked back bacon or 3 slices smoked streaky bacon
Aromatic wood – e.g. shop-bought hickory or mesquite
    (available in chunks or small chips) or 'green' apple, oak or
    vine wood.

Remove and discard the giblets, and then rinse and dry the chicken. Lay the bacon slices across the top of the chicken. Roast over a medium to high heat. For a dramatic colour and distinctive flavour, drop small pieces of aromatic mixture on the hot fuel roughly half way during cooking. For more or less colour and flavour, add the aromatic mixture either earlier or later. Remember to pre-soak aromatic mixtures in water before adding to the hot coals or rocks.

Honeyed Chicken Kebabs

Serves 4

1 garlic clove, crushed
½ tsp ground ginger
½ tsp ground coriander
3 tbs clear honey
2 tbs olive oil, plus extra
2 tbs dry vermouth
2 tbs soy sauce
juice of half a lime
500 g (1 lb) chicken breast or thighs, skinned

Mix all the ingredients except the chicken together in a large shallow dish. Cut the chicken into 1–2 cm (½–¾-inch) cubes and put them in the marinade. Leave for several hours, or overnight in the refrigerator.

Thread the chicken on oiled skewers and grill over a medium heat for 10–15 minutes, turning frequently. Baste the chicken with the marinade once towards the end of the cooking.

Duckling with Orange

Serves 3–4

1.75–2.25 kg (4–5 lb) duckling
1 small glass dry white wine
juice of ½ a lemon
62.5 g packet Black Pepper butter
4 medium-size oranges, peeled and sliced
salt

Remove the giblets, and then wash and dry the duckling, inside and out. Season the bird with the white wine, lemon juice and salt. Leave overnight in a cool place.

When ready to cook, rub the flavoured butter over the duckling. Roast over a medium to high heat. After 30 minutes, prick the skin of the thigh and breast areas with a large needle and baste frequently with the juices of the duck and flavoured butter. Cook for about 2 hours, or until tender.

Cut the duckling into portions and place them on a hot serving dish. Skim the fat from the juices and pour the liquid over the meat portions. Decorate the dish with the sliced oranges and serve immediately.

Duckling with Orange
Buttered Breast of Chicken

Buttered Breast of Chicken*

Serves 8

8 large chicken breasts, about 250 g (8 oz) each
175 g (6 oz) plain flour
3 × 62.5 g packets Lemon and Parsley butter or Herbs and
*   Garlic butter, melted*
softened butter for basting
salt and pepper

Slice each chicken breast across in two. Rinse and dry the
chicken thoroughly. Season the flour and place it in a plastic
bag. Dip the chicken pieces, one at a time, in the melted
butter, and then shake each in the plastic bag to coat it
thoroughly. Place the chicken on a greased grill 13–25 cm
(5–10 inches) above a high heat. Baste with the softened
butter. Cook for about 10 minutes on each side or until the
juices run clear when pierced with a fork.

Barbecued Pheasant*

Serves 2–4

1 plump well hung pheasant, about 750 g–1 kg (1½–2 lb)
3 tbs butter
3 slices streaky bacon
freshly ground black pepper

Carefully wipe the pheasant inside and out with a damp
cloth. Cover the wing tips and the knuckle end of the legs
with foil. Spread a generous layer of butter over the outside
of the bird and wrap the slices of bacon around it. Season
the bird with the ground pepper.

Roast over a medium heat for 1–1¼ hours. Remove the
bacon during the last 15 minutes so the breast can brown
nicely.

Spit-roasted Venison

Serves 6–8

1.75–2.25 kg (4–5 lb) saddle or loin of venison, trimmed of fat
125 g (4 oz) salt pork, cut into thin strips
2 garlic cloves, slivered
175 g (6 oz) clear honey
150 ml (¼ pint) soy sauce
300 ml (½ pint) orange juice
150 ml (¼ pint) tomato ketchup
300 ml (½ pint) wine vinegar
1 tsp salt
½ tsp freshly ground black pepper
1 tsp dry mustard
½ tsp paprika

Wipe the roast with a damp cloth. Make slits in the roast and
lard generously with the salt pork and garlic. In a small pan,
combine the honey, soy sauce, orange juice, tomato ketchup, wine vinegar, salt, pepper, mustard and paprika. Position
the roast on the spit and insert a meat thermometer in the
thickest part of the meat. Brush on the basting sauce and
roast over a medium heat, basting occasionally, until the
thermometer registers 60°C/140°F for rare meat to 85°C/185°F
for well done meat.

FISH AND SHELLFISH RECIPES

➤ Grilling time for fish depends on its thickness, not its weight. In general, allow 10 minutes for each 2.5 cm (1 inch) of thickness.

➤ Fish is cooked when it flakes easily with a fork. It should be opaque with no pink near the backbone, and juices should be clear.

➤ Shellfish only needs minimal cooking. When it looks opaque, it is ready.

Grilled Mackerel in a Cheesy Crust

Serves 4

4 × 375 g (12 oz) mackerel
25 g (1 oz) dry white breadcrumbs
50 g (2 oz) parmesan cheese, grated
2 garlic cloves, minced
1/4 tsp salt
1/8 tsp black pepper
4 tbs sunflower oil
4 tbs lemon juice
1 tbs chopped parsley
1/2 tsp dried basil

Clean and bone the mackerel and, if desired, remove the heads. Combine the breadcrumbs, parmesan cheese, half of the garlic, salt and pepper and mix thoroughly.

Prepare a basting sauce by mixing together the sunflower oil, lemon juice, chopped parsley, basil and remaining garlic.

Dip each fish in the basting sauce and then into the cheese and crumb mixture. Place the fish in the fish broiler or flesh-side down on a well oiled grill over a medium heat; cook for about 5 minutes. Carefully turn the fish and brush the basting sauce over the upper side. Baste occasionally for a further 8–10 minutes, or until the skin is crisp and the flesh can be flaked easily with a fork.

Marinated Fish Steaks

Serves 4

4 × 2.5–4 cm (1–1½-inch) thick fresh or frozen halibut or
  haddock steaks
Seafare Marinade (see p. 87)
75 g (3 oz) butter, melted
½ tsp salt
¼ tsp pepper
1 tbs lemon juice

Place the fish in a shallow dish, pour the Seafare Marinade over them and leave for about 30 minutes, turning once.

If using a fish broiler, cook over a medium heat for about 10 minutes, brushing the fish occasionally with the melted butter mixed with the salt and pepper and lemon juice.

If a hinged broiler is unavailable, tear off four pieces of 46 cm (18-inch) heavy-duty foil and brush melted butter on the polished surface of each piece. Drain the fish and place one portion on each of the buttered surfaces, and then season with salt and pepper. Combine the remainder of the melted butter with the lemon juice and brush over the fish. Fold the foil over and secure the edges tightly.

Place the packages on the grill over a medium heat and cook for about 20 minutes, or until the fish flakes easily with a fork.

Tandoori Fish

Serves 2–3

75 g (3 oz) butter, melted
½ tsp ground nutmeg
1½ tsp ground cinnamon
1½ tsp ground coriander
juice of 1½ lemons, strained
1 × 1 kg (2 lb) whole white fish, such as haddock or cod
1 medium-size onion, chopped finely
4 garlic cloves, minced
2.5 cm (1-inch) piece of fresh ginger root, peeled and chopped finely
1 tsp ground cumin
¼ tsp chilli powder
1 tsp ground fennel
½ tsp paprika
1 tsp salt
¼ tsp freshly ground black pepper
150 ml (¼ pint) yogurt

For the basting sauce, combine the melted butter, nutmeg, ½ tsp cinnamon, ½ tsp coriander, and a third of the lemon juice. Blend well and put aside.

Clean the fish, and then make three diagonal incisions on each side. Put the onion, garlic, ginger, cumin, rest of the coriander, chilli powder, rest of the cinnamon, fennel, paprika, salt, pepper and the rest of the lemon juice in a food processor (or use a pestle and mortar) and blend them to a paste. Stir in the yogurt. Rub the paste on the inside and outside of the fish and leave it in a cool place for 3–4 hours.

Mount the fish on a spit or within a spit-mounted double-hinged fish broiler, or grill using a large hinged fish broiler. Cook the fish over a moderate heat, basting frequently with the basting sauce, for 15 minutes if spit-roasting or 7–8 minutes per side if grilling.

Garlic-kissed Prawn Kebabs

Serves 6 (Pictured on front cover)

12 large raw Pacific or Dublin Bay Prawns
4 tbs lemon juice
2 tbs finely chopped parsley
300 ml (½ pint) olive oil
3 garlic cloves, crushed
¼ tsp freshly ground black pepper

To prepare the prawns, pull the legs away leaving the shell and tail intact. Snip the shells open along their backs. Remove the dark vein after cutting carefully into the back flesh (use the tip of a knife to remove the vein). Rinse the prawns in cold water.

Mix the lemon juice, parsley, olive oil, garlic and pepper. Marinate the prawns at room temperature for 1–2 hours. Thread the prawns on 6 bamboo or wooden skewers.

Grill the prawn kebabs over a medium to high heat, basting once on each side, for 4–5 minutes per side, or until the flesh is white and opaque. Be careful not to overcook. Serve in their shells, with a little of the marinade poured over them, if desired.

Whole Salmon With Special Rice Stuffing*

Serves 8–14

1 × 1.75–3 kg (4–7 lb) salmon
6 tbs butter, plus extra
1 small onion, chopped finely
125 g (4 oz) celery, chopped finely
250 g (8 oz) American long grain rice
1 tsp grated lemon peel
juice of 1 lemon
1/2 tsp dried thyme
1/2 tsp dried basil
600 ml (1 pint) water
125 g (4 oz) closed cup mushrooms, sliced thinly
1/2 tsp garlic salt
1 tsp salt
1/4 tsp freshly ground black pepper
1 medium-size grapefruit

Wipe the fish inside and out with a damp cloth and pat dry with paper towels. Remove the head and tail if desired.

For the stuffing, melt 3 tbs butter in a heavy pan. Add the finely chopped onion and celery and cook over a medium-high heat for about 4 minutes, until the vegetables are soft. Add the rice and cook for a further minute. Add the lemon peel, lemon juice, thyme, basil and water and bring the mixture to the boil. Stir once, lower heat to simmer (if using a charcoal barbecue, move pan to a cooler area or raise the grill) and cover the pan. Cook for about 20 minutes, or until all the liquid is absorbed.

Meanwhile, melt 3 tbs butter in a separate pan and cook the sliced mushrooms for about 5 minutes, until they are soft. Add to the cooked rice along with the garlic salt, salt and pepper.

Grilled Mussels
Whole Salmon with Special Rice Stuffing

Make an aluminium pan (see p. 25) large enough for the fish. Brush the surface of the pan with melted butter. Slice the grapefruit very thinly and place a line of overlapping slices down the centre of the greased pan. Lightly pack the stuffing into the fish and sew it together with thin string. Brush the fish generously with melted butter and lay it on the grapefruit. Arrange the remaining slices on top of the fish. Wrap excess stuffing in foil and heat it with the salmon.

Roast the salmon over a medium heat until the flesh flakes easily with a fork and the juices run clear. Measure the thickness of the stuffed fish. Allow 10 minutes per 2.5 cm (1-inch) thickness.

When cooked, use one or two fish slices to transfer it on to a warm serving platter. Remove the skin and cut along the backbone for serving. Use a spatula to lift off individual servings and serve with the special rice stuffing.

The amount of stuffing in this recipe is calculated for a 3 kg (7 lb) salmon. For a 1.75–2.25 kg (4–5 lb) fish, halve the stuffing ingredients.

Grilled Mussels

Serves 4

40–50 mussels
a large bunch of dried herbs, such as rosemary, thyme, etc.

Scrape, scrub and wash the mussels carefully. Place them on the grill about 15 cm (6 inches) above a medium to high heat. Scatter the dried herbs on the coals throughout the short cooking period. When the mussels have opened fully, leave them on the grill for another minute and then serve immediately. Discard any mussels that do not open.

Red Mullet Grilled with Fennel

Serves 4

4 large or 8 small red mullet
1 tbs melted butter
2 tbs sunflower oil
$\frac{1}{2}$ tsp peppercorns, cracked
3 large bay leaves, each broken in 4
2 tbs dry white wine
2 garlic cloves, chopped finely
1 tbs chopped fennel leaves

Clean the fish, leaving the liver (considered a great delicacy) intact. Mix together the rest of the ingredients and pour over the fish. Marinate for about 1 hour.

Reserving the marinade, drain the fish and cook for 5–8 minutes on each side, depending on the size of the fish. Baste two or three times during cooking with the marinade.

Grilled Sardines with Herb Butter

Serves 4–6

16 fresh sardines
3 tbs sunflower oil
Herb Butter (see p. 91)
salt and pepper

Clean and dry the fish and brush lightly with the oil. Season the fish with salt and pepper. Place the fish on a well oiled grill and cook over a high heat for about 10 minutes, turning once. Serve at once with pats of herb butter.

Frozen sardines may be used, but thaw before cooking.

Grilled Trout with Herb Butter

Serves 4

4 × 375 g (12 oz) trout
3 tbs olive oil
1 medium-size onion, chopped finely
1 tsp French mustard
1 tbs minced chives
2 tbs minced dill
1 tsp salt
1 tbs lemon juice
1/2 tsp pepper
2 tbs melted butter
Herb Butter (see p. 91)

Clean and bone the trout and, if desired, remove the heads. Flatten out the fish and place them flesh-side down in a shallow dish.

Combine the olive oil, onion, mustard, chives, dill, salt, lemon juice and pepper and mix thoroughly. Pour this marinade over the fish and leave in the refrigerator for about an hour; turn the fish once.

Place the fish, flesh-side down, on an oiled grill over a medium to high heat and cook for about 4 minutes. Turn the fish over and brush melted butter over the cooked side. Continue grilling for another 6 minutes, or until the skin of the trout is crisp and the flesh is white and can easily be flaked. Spread the herb butter over the fish just before serving.

VEGETABLE AND FRUIT RECIPES

➤ Most vegetables can be grilled directly on the barbecue if basted frequently.

➤ New and old potatoes, sweet potatoes, yams and whole onions can be cooked directly on the hot coals. Turn frequently. They are ready when they feel soft. Remove the charred skins.

➤ Vegetables come out beautifully when cooked in foil. Place 4 portions on a large square of heavy-duty foil, add a knob of butter (flavoured if desired) and 1 tbs of water. Seal tightly and place on the grill for about 20 minutes.

➤ Most fruit can be grilled on the barbecue as long as it is marinated or basted.

Orange Butter-glazed Carrots

Serves 4–6

1 kg (2 lb) new carrots, scrubbed or scraped
2 oranges
75 g (3 oz) butter
3 tbs brown sugar

Parboil the carrots in salted water until just tender but still crisp. Drain well. Grate the rind from the oranges and extract the juice. Combine the orange rind, orange juice, butter and brown sugar in a saucepan and heat gently until the sugar has dissolved. Bring the mixture to the boil, and then simmer gently for 5 minutes. Dip the carrots in the mixture, and then barbecue them over a medium heat, turning and basting occasionally for 5 minutes.

Vegetable Kebabs

Serves 6   (Pictured on front cover)

6 small or new potatoes
6 small onions
12 closed cup button mushrooms, wiped
2 green peppers
50 g (2 oz) butter, melted
½ tsp garlic salt
¼ tsp freshly ground black pepper
6 small tomatoes

Peel or scrub the potatoes and onions and cook them separately in lightly salted boiling water until they are barely tender. Remove the stems from the mushrooms and wipe the caps. De-seed the peppers and cut into 12 pieces. Drain the onion and potatoes, and thread all but the tomatoes alternately on the oiled skewers.

Blend the melted butter, garlic salt, and pepper together and brush the kebabs generously with the mixture. Cook with the grill set about 10–13 cm (4–5 inches) above a medium to high heat. After 5 minutes, add a tomato to each skewer, turn the kebabs over and brush with more of the flavoured butter. Cook for another 5 minutes.

Buttered and Grilled Corn on the Cob

1 ear of young sweetcorn per person
softened butter
salt
Garlic Butter (see p. 91) for method 3
1 rasher fat bacon per person, for method 4

Method 1
Strip away the husks and silk. Spread the sweetcorn with butter and season to taste with salt. Place on a grill 15–23 cm (6–9 inches) above a medium heat and cook for 15–20 minutes, turning and basting regularly with the remaining butter.

Method 2
Remove the corn husks and silk and rinse well in salted iced water. Place each cob on a sheet of extra-thick aluminium foil and brush with 15 g (½ oz) of softened butter. Sprinkle 1 tbs water over the corn, wrap securely and place in the barbecue coals (or on top of lava rock if using a gas barbecue) for about 15 minutes, turning several times.

Method 3
Remove the outer corn husk, turn back the inner husks and remove the silk and rinse well in salted iced water. Brush the corn generously with Garlic Butter. Replace husks over cob and hold them in place with hoops of fine wire (position the wire near each end and in the centre). Cook on the barbecue grill over a high heat for about 20 minutes, turning every 3–5 minutes. To serve, cut the wire and remove the husks (good heat-resistant gloves are useful for this job).

Method 4
Strip away the husks and silk. Remove the rind from a rasher of fat bacon, wrap the bacon around the corn and secure with cocktail sticks previously soaked in cold water. Grill over high heat for about 20 minutes, turning frequently, or until the bacon is crisp and the uncovered areas of the corn are golden brown.

Dunk-in-dip Vegetables

Serves 6

250 g (8 oz) Spring Onion salad dressing
1 tbs finely chopped black olives
1 tbs finely chopped cooked ham
250 g (8 oz) Herb and Garlic salad dressing
2 tbs chopped prawns
250 g (8 oz) Yogurt and Chive salad dressing
2 tbs finely chopped hard-boiled egg
Vegetable Kebabs (see p. 70)

In one bowl, mix the Spring Onion salad dressing with the
black olives and cooked ham. In a second bowl, combine the
Herb and Garlic salad dressing with the chopped prawns. In
a third bowl, stir the Yogurt and Chive salad dressing and
the chopped egg together. Chill all the dips while you
prepare and grill the Vegetable Kebabs. Remove the kebabs
from the skewers and dunk the chunks of vegetables in the
dips.

Stuffed Tomatoes

Serves 4

2 large firm tomatoes
3 tbs fresh white breadcrumbs
2 tbs finely chopped parsley
⅛ tsp garlic powder
25 g (1 oz) grated cheese, Cheddar, mozzarella or to choice
2 tbs butter, softened
a pinch of dried basil

Cut the tomatoes in half lengthways and scrape out the seeds using a teaspoon. Combine the remaining ingredients and lightly pack the mixture into the tomato cavities.

Position the tomatoes, cut-side up, on a grill over a medium to high heat. Cook for about 10 minutes, or until the tomatoes are heated through and the cheese has melted.

Judy's Gem Squash

Serves 1–2

1 gem squash
50 g (2 oz) butter
salt
freshly ground black pepper

Remove the stem, and then cut the squash in half crossways and scoop out the seeds. Place half the butter in the centre of each half-squash. Season the squash with a light sprinkling of salt and a generous amount of freshly ground black pepper.

Centre each half on a square of heavy-duty foil roughly three times the diameter of the fruit. Bring the four corners of the foil together into a pyramid shape. Seal the package by loosely folding over the foil edges where they come together. Keep the package in an upright position and grill over a high heat for about 15 minutes or roast for 25–30 minutes.

Note: As an alternative method of cooking, brush oil all over the skin of the whole squash and nestle it in hot coals. Roast the squash for 50–60 minutes, turning occasionally. Cut the cooked squash in half crossways, scoop out the seeds and butter and season as above.

Baked Potatoes

Universally popular, baked potatoes are ideal for barbecues. Complete with scrumptious toppings or stuffings they are a meal in themselves. They make a good contrast to the meat, are perfect for the oft-forgotten vegetarian and the possibilities for fillings are endless. Use even-size medium to large baking potatoes such as Maris Piper, King Edward, Pentland Ivory and Golden Wonder. Scrub well, pat dry and prick them deeply all over with a fork. Brush with oil and season with salt and pepper or generously with your favourite barbecue spice. Wrap them tightly in foil. If using charcoal, place them directly on the coals (preferably around the perimeter). For gas, place them on the food grill on a medium to high setting. Turn several times during cooking. Medium-size potatoes will take 45–60 minutes and large potatoes will take 60–70 minutes. They are ready when they feel soft. The recipes below are enough for 4 potatoes.

Chicken and Chive-flavoured Sour Cream Filling

4 tbs sour cream
2 tbs chicken stock granules (beef granules may be used instead)
1 tbs finely chopped fresh chives

Pickle, Sausage and Cheese Filling

3 tbs sweet pickle, chopped
4 cooked pork chipolata sausages, sliced thinly
75 g (3 oz) grated Cheddar cheese
25 g (1 oz) butter

Cream Cheese and Avocado Filling

125 g (4 oz) cream cheese
1 medium-size avocado, chopped roughly

Bacon and Cream Cheese Filling

125 g (4 oz) cream cheese
175 g (6 oz) grilled back bacon, chopped roughly
50 g (2 oz) butter
2 tbs finely chopped fresh chives

Poor Man's Caviar and Cream Filling

150 ml (¼ pint) sour cream
1 tbs finely chopped fresh chives
4 tsp black or red lumpfish roe

Gingered Pears

Serves 4

4 tsp unsalted butter
2 tsp castor sugar, plus extra
2 tsp ground ginger
a pinch of cinnamon or nutmeg
4 medium to large Comice pears
juice of 1 lemon
single cream (optional)

Cream together the butter, sugar, ground ginger and cinnamon or nutmeg. If necessary, trim the base of the pears so that they stand upright, leaving the stalks intact. Stand each pear one at a time in a saucer containing the lemon juice. Brush each pear liberally with the juice. Cut off the top of each pear about 2.5 cm (1-inch) below the base of the stalk and reserve. Remove the cores, taking care not to break through the base. Stuff the prepared mixture into the cavities.

Replace the tops and stand each pear on a lightly greased 25 cm (10-inch) square piece of foil. Brush the remaining lemon juice over the pears and dust with castor sugar. Gather and twist the foil at the base of the stalks to secure. Stand the pears in a shallow baking tin or double-thickness foil drip pan (see p. 25). Cook for about 40 minutes over a medium heat. The pears are ready if they feel soft when gently squeezed. Remove them by the stalks. Be careful not to burn yourself. Serve the pears with single cream if desired.

Spiced Barbecue Bananas

Serves 4

4 medium-ripe, firm bananas
lemon juice
4 pinches of ground cinnamon
4 pinches of ground ginger (optional)
2 tsp clear honey or 4 tsp brown sugar
4 tsp butter or margarine

Peel the bananas and place each in the centre of a 23 × 15 cm (9 × 6-inch) sheet of heavy-duty foil. Squeeze or brush lemon juice generously over each banana. Dust them with ground cinnamon, and with ground ginger if desired. Dribble a ½ tsp of clear honey or sprinkle 1 tsp of the brown sugar along each banana. Position 1 tsp of butter at the base of each banana.

Lap the long edges of the foil together, leaving plenty of room for air, squeeze the ends of the package closed, and turn upwards. The end result should look something like a gondola.

If cooking over a high heat allow about 5 minutes. To be on the safe side, check one situated in the hottest area of the grill after 4 minutes.

If it appears to be softening slightly at the base, remove all the bananas immediately. The bananas will continue to cook in their packets. Be careful not to let them overcook. To save on washing up, serve the bananas straight from their packets. Pass around paper plates or serviettes to protect guests' hands.

Vanilla ice cream goes very well with the bananas.

Bread and Fruit Kebabs

Serves 6 (Pictured on front cover)

2 pears, peeled and cored
melon balls from 1 small melon
juice of 2 lemons
2 oranges, cut in 1 cm (½-inch) slices
1 small pineapple, peeled and cored, or tinned chunks
12 large firm strawberries
3 firm medium-size bananas, each cut in 4
125 g (4 oz) castor sugar
3 tbs liqueur of your choice
4 tbs white wine
1 white loaf, with crusts removed
125 g (4 oz) butter, melted

Cut the pears into large chunks and place them with the melon balls in the lemon juice. Quarter each orange slice and cut the fresh pineapple into 2.5 cm (1–inch) cubes. Place all the fruit in a large bowl and add half of the sugar, the liqueur and the white wine. Mix gently and leave the fruit to macerate in a cool place for 20–30 minutes.

Cut the bread into 2.5 cm (1-inch) cubes and brush each with melted butter. Toss them in a bowl with the rest of the sugar, ensuring that the bread is evenly coated.

Thread a selection of the fruit with a couple of pieces of bread on long, oiled metal skewers. Set the grill 10–15 cm (4–6 inches) above a medium heat. Turn, and dust occasionally with more sugar. Cook for about 5–6 minutes until the kebabs are evenly browned and caramelised. If desired, the marinade can be sprinkled over the kebabs before eating.

Brenda Mary's Pineapple Flambé

Serves 4

1 fresh pineapple, or 8 slices of canned pineapple
6 tbs clear honey
2 tbs white rum

If using a fresh pineapple, remove the skin and cut out the hard fibrous centre. Slice the pineapple into eight rings. Grill the fresh or tinned rings over a high heat for about 2–3 minutes on each side. Baste frequently with the honey.

Place the cooked pineapple rings on a serving dish and sprinkle them with the rum. Set the rum alight and serve immediately with cream or ice cream.

Spiced and Stuffed Apples

Serves 6

6 medium-size cooking apples
125 g (4 oz) brown sugar
2 tsp ground cinnamon
40 g (1½ oz) walnuts, chopped finely
40 g (1½ oz) raisins, chopped finely
6 tsp butter

Wash and core the apples. Place each on a piece of doubled aluminium foil. Combine the brown sugar, cinnamon, walnuts and raisins and fill the centres of the apples with the mixture. Top each apple with a teaspoon of butter, and then wrap the edges of the foil securely. Barbecue the apples on the grill over a medium heat for 40–50 minutes. The apples are cooked when soft. Serve them topped with whipped cream or vanilla ice cream.

Brenda Mary's Pineapple Flambé

BASIC RECIPES AND ACCOMPANIMENTS

Sweet and Sour Sauce

Makes 450 ml (¾ pint)

150 ml (¼ pint) dry white wine
1½ tbs white wine vinegar
1½ tbs sunflower oil
300 ml (½ pint) crushed pineapple (undrained)
1 tbs soy sauce
1 tsp lemon juice
¼ tsp garlic salt
½ tsp dry mustard
1½ tbs brown sugar
¾ tbs chopped onion (optional)

Combine all the ingredients, mix well, and simmer in a saucepan for about 10–15 minutes. Use to baste poultry, pork, lamb, ribs and fish steaks.

Spicy Orange Sauce

Makes 450 ml (¾ pint)

4 tbs soy sauce
6 tbs orange juice
6 tbs soft brown sugar
8 tbs dry white wine
½ tsp dry mustard
½ tsp paprika
2 dashes of Tabasco Pepper sauce
1 shallot, chopped finely
a pinch of ground cinnamon

3 tbs water
2 tsp cornflour
salt and pepper

Mix together all but the cornflour and salt and pepper. Bring slowly to the boil, stirring continuously. Simmer for 5–6 minutes. Add a small amount of water to the cornflour to make a smooth paste and then add to the simmering sauce. Keep simmering until the sauce thickens. Season with salt and pepper. Serve with chicken and pork.

Wild Bill's Barbecue Sauce

Makes 900 ml (1½ pints)

3 tbs Worcestershire sauce
1 tsp chilli powder
1 tsp dry mustard
1 tsp salt
1 tsp freshly ground pepper
4 tbs honey
300 ml (½ pint) chilli sauce
300 ml (½ pint) tomato sauce
2 dashes of Tabasco Pepper sauce
3 tbs wine vinegar
6 tbs water
3 tbs tarragon vinegar

Mix all the ingredients together; add a little more water if it is too thick. This sauce is particularly good for basting ribs during the last few minutes of cooking.

Indonesian Sauce

Makes 450 ml (¾ pint)

1 tbs groundnut oil
4 tbs smooth peanut butter
150 ml (¼ pint) tomato ketchup
3 tbs Worcestershire sauce
garlic powder to taste
¼ tsp salt

Heat the oil gently in a pan and add the peanut butter. Continue heating gently, stirring occasionally until the peanut butter begins to thicken and darkens slightly. Remove from the heat immediately and stir in the tomato ketchup and Worcestershire sauce. Season to taste with the garlic powder and salt. Leave to stand for 2 hours for the flavours to blend. Reheat gently, and add a little water if the sauce is too thick.

Serve with barbecued chicken, seafood and steaks; it can also be used to baste chicken.

Red Wine Marinade

Makes 300 ml (½ pint)

300 ml (½ pint) dry red wine
1 tsp dried whole basil or oregano
2 garlic cloves, crushed
1 tsp salt
2 tbs wine vinegar
1½ tbs melted butter or sunflower oil

Combine all the ingredients and heat in a saucepan until the marinade starts to simmer. Remove from the heat immediately, cover the pan and allow to stand for about an hour. Pour over pork or beef and marinate for 2–5 hours, according to taste.

Indonesian Sauce

Teriyaki Marinade

Makes 150 ml (¼ pint)

1½ tbs clear honey
1½ tbs sunflower oil
4 tbs soy sauce
¾ tbs dry red wine or red wine vinegar
1 tsp freshly grated ginger or a pinch of ground ginger
1 garlic clove, crushed

Combine all the ingredients and pour over the food.

Refrigerate, turning occasionally. Marinate chicken and spare-ribs for 4–8 hours, beef for 8 hours, and fish for 2–4 hours. This marinade can also be used as a baste.

Mint with Honey Marinade

Makes 450 ml (¾ pint)

150 ml (¼ pint) dry white wine
4 tbs clear honey
2 tsp chopped fresh mint
1 tbs wine vinegar
1 garlic clove, crushed
1 tsp salt

Combine all the ingredients until well blended. Leave to stand for about an hour before use, for the flavours to mingle. Marinate lamb or chicken for 1 hour.

Universal Barbecue Marinade

Makes 150 ml (¼ pint)

3 tbs dry sherry
2 tbs soy sauce
3 tbs sunflower oil
1 tsp Worcestershire sauce
1 tsp garlic powder
freshly ground black pepper

This marinade can be used for meat, poultry or fish. Combine all the ingredients and mix well. Pour the marinade over meat, poultry, or fish and refrigerate, turning occasionally. Allow 3–5 hours for steaks, (depending on thickness), 24–48 hours for roasts, (depending on roast size), and 2 hours for poultry and salmon. This marinade can also be used as a basting sauce.

Seafare Marinade

Makes 150 ml (¼ pint)

150 ml (¼ pint) dry white wine
3 tbs sunflower oil
1 tsp paprika
½ tsp salt
⅛ tsp freshly ground black pepper
1 tsp sugar
¾ tbs minced parsley

Combine all the ingredients and pour over seafood. Marinate for 1 hour.

Flavoured Butters

A few flavoured butters to accompany barbecued food is an easy way to add extra flavour and piquancy. It also lets everyone choose the flavour they want. You can make your own flavoured butters from scratch, but for extra convenience there are now high-quality flavoured butters on the market. You can use these pre-flavoured butters as the base for any of these recipes (adjusting the seasoning to taste). You can also use them to baste barbecuing meat, chicken, fish, shellfish and vegetables; to add to vegetables cooked in foil; and to top off baked potatoes. In fact, you can add them anywhere you want more savoury flavour. Beat the butter until soft. Add the rest of the ingredients and mix well. Chill thoroughly before serving. Flavoured butter can be kept in the refrigerator for 7–10 days.

Black Pepper, Red Wine and Spring Onion Butter
2 tbs finely chopped spring onion
1 tbs red wine
2 × 62.5 g packets Black Pepper butter
For red meat.

Herby Garlicky Caper Butter
2 tbs finely chopped capers
2 × 62.5 g packets Herbs and Garlic butter
For white and dark meat, and fish.

Blue Cheese and Port Butter
2 tbs port
2 × 62.5 g packets Blue Cheese butter
For vegetables, red meat and game (the port can be replaced with madeira).

Blue Cheese and Port Butter
Garlic Butter
Lemon and Parsley White Wine and Olive Butter
Herby Garlicky Caper Butter
Black Pepper, Red Wine and Spring Onion Butter

Lemon and Parsley White Wine and Olive Butter

1 tbs dry white wine
1 tbs very finely chopped black olives
2 × 62.5 g packets Lemon and Parsley butter

For light and dark meat (gherkins may be used instead of olives).

Tarragon and Parsley Butter

1/2 tsp grated lemon peel
2 tsp lemon juice
1 tbs finely chopped parsley
1/4 tsp salt
1/4 tsp dried crushed tarragon
125 g (4 oz) butter

For red meat, especially steaks.

Orange and Honey Butter

1 tbs orange juice
1 tbs grated orange rind
1 tbs clear honey
2 tsp finely chopped parsley
125 g (4 oz) butter

For lamb, duck, and chicken.

Maître D'Hotel Butter

2 tsp finely chopped parsley
1/4 tsp salt
2 tsp lemon juice
1/4 tsp thyme
a pinch of freshly ground black pepper
125 g (4 oz) butter

For vegetables and fish, or as a baste for chicken.

Anchovy Butter

1 1/2 tbs anchovy paste
1/4 tsp lemon juice
125 g (4 oz) butter

For seafood.

Garlic Butter

1 garlic clove, finely minced
1 1/2 tbs chopped parsley
125 g (4 oz) butter

For seafood, red meat, French bread and vegetables.

Herb Butter

1/2 tsp dried tarragon or dried rosemary
1 tbs finely chopped chives
1 tbs finely chopped parsley
1/4 tsp salt
a pinch of freshly ground black pepper
125 g (4 oz) butter
For poultry, seafood and vegetables.

Cheesy Torpedo

Serves 4–6

1 French loaf
125 g (4 oz) Garlic Butter (see above)
175 g (6 oz) Cheddar cheese, grated

Cut the loaf in half, lengthways. Spread the garlic butter generously over the two cut surfaces. Sprinkle the grated cheese evenly over one buttered surface and press the two halves together. Spread any remaining garlic butter over the surface of the loaf, and then wrap it up securely in a double thickness of heavy-duty foil, dull side out.

Heat the 'torpedo' on a grill set 10–13 cm (4–5 inches) over a medium heat for 10–12 minutes or for approximately 15–20 minutes if using the warming grill of a barbecue; turn two or three times. If using a covered barbecue, roast for about 15 minutes.

BARBECUING TIME-CHARTS

Roasting (for covered barbecues)

Food	Cut	Degree of cooking	Internal temperature (°F)	Approx minutes per pound
Beef	rib roast	rare	140	18–20
		medium	160	20–25
		well done	170	25–30
	sirloin		140–170	25–30
	rump/rolled		150–170	25–30
Lamb	leg	rare	140	18–22
		medium	160	22–28
		well done	170	28–33
	crown roast	rare	140	28–33
		medium	160	33–38
		well done	170	38–43
	shoulder	medium	160	22–28
		well done	170	28–33
Pork	loin	well done	185	25–30
	fresh ham	well done	185	20–25
	crown	well done	185	25–30
Veal	loin	well done	185	20–25
	leg	well done	185	20–25
	shoulder	well done	185	20–25
Poultry	chicken	well done	185	18–20
	turkey	well done	185	12–20★
	duckling	well done	185	15–20

★Cooking times will vary greatly according to weight of bird

Spit-roasting

Food	Cut	Size or weight	Recommended heat	Approx cooking time in hours*		
				rare	medium	well done
Beef	rump (rolled)	3–5 lb	medium	140°F 1½–2	160°F 2¼–3	190°F 3–4
	sirloin	5–6 lb	medium/hot	1¼–1¾	2¼–3	3–4
	rolled rib	4–6 lb	medium/hot	2–2½	2¼–3	3¼–4½
Lamb	Leg	3½–8 lb	medium	140°F 1–1¼	160°F 1½–2	180°F 2–3¼
	rolled shoulder	3–6 lb	medium	1–1¼	1½–2	2–3¼
Pork	Shoulder	3–6 lb	medium			185°F 2–3
	loin	3–5 lb	medium			2–3
	spareribs	2–4 lb	medium/hot			1–1¾
	fresh ham	5–8 lb	medium			3½–4½
Poultry	chicken	2½–5 lb	medium			190°F 1–1½
	turkey	10–18 lb	medium			2–4
	duckling	4–6 lb	medium			1–2
Veal	leg	5–8 lb	medium			190°F 2–3
	rolled shoulder	3–5 lb	medium			1½–2½
	loin	5–6 lb	medium			1½–2¼
Fish	large, whole	5–10 lb	low/medium			120–130°F 1–1¼
	small, whole	1½–4 lb	low/medium			½–1

*For accuracy use a meat thermometer and cook to the internal temperatures given in the chart.

Grilling

Food	Cut	Size or weight	Recommended heat	Approx cooking time (each side) in minutes		
				rare	medium	well done
Beef	steak	1 inch	hot	5-6	7-8	10-12
	steak*	1½ inches	hot	6-7	9-10	12-15
	flank steak	whole	hot	4-5†		7-10
	hamburger	1 inch	medium	3-4	5-6	10-12
	skewer		hot	4-5	6-8	
Lamb	chops	1 inch	medium	5-6	7-8	10
	skewer		medium	5-6	7-8	10
Pork	chops	¾-1 inch	medium			18-20
	spare-ribs	whole	low-medium			1-1¼ hrs
	skewer		medium			15-20
Poultry	chicken	split	medium			35-45
	duck	split	medium	5-6	10-11	25
Veal	steaks or chops	1 inch	medium			9-12
	skewer		medium			10-15
Fish	steak	½ inch	medium			3-4
	steak	1 inch	medium			5-7
	fillets	¾ inch	medium			5-7
Lobster	split	1-1½ lb	medium/hot			14-15
Ham	slice	1 inch	medium			15-20

*If steaks are two inches or more thick you can use a meat thermometer. Steak is rare at 130°F, well done at 170°F.

† Maximum cooking time for meat to be tender.

INDEX

Jim Marks' personal and commercial interest in barbecuing goes back to the late sixties. In his ceaseless campaign to promote the joys of barbecuing, he has participated in numerous radio phone-ins, appeared frequently on television – including BBC 2's 'Food and Drink' programme, and has written several books and articles on the subject. In addition, he has given hundreds of barbecue demonstrations throughout the United Kingdom. Since becoming a full-time freelance consultant, he has spent most spring and summer days in this pursuit.

Jim Marks' expertise, which has earned him the title of 'Mr Barbecue', is reflected in the content of *Better Barbecuing*.

Design and Layout: Ken Vail Graphic Design
Photography: Sue Jorgensen
Home Economist: Berit Vinegrad
Stylist: Maria Kelly
Illustrations: David Butler

Typesetting: Goodfellow and Egan
Printed and bound by Springbourne Press, Basildon, Essex